Corpus Christi is dedicated to my partner, Gary Bonasorte

TERRENCE McNALLY

Corpus Christi
A Play

Grove Press
New York

Published simultaneously in Canada
Printed in the United States of America

FIRST EDITION

Library of Congress Cataloging-in-Publication Data

McNally, Terrence,
Corpus Christi : a play / Terrence McNally.
p. cm.
ISBN 0-8021-3635-4
1. Gay men—Texas—Drama. I. Title.
PS3563.A323C67   1999
812'.54—dc21   99-13624
CIP

Grove Press
841 Broadway
New York, NY 10003

99 00 01 02   10 9 8 7 6 5 4 3 2 1

Preface

I'm a playwright, not a theologian.

But it would have been just as naïve of me to think that I could write a play about a young gay man who would come to be identified as a Christ figure without stirring up a protest as it would to think I could write a play about Jesus Christ Himself in which He would come to be identified as a young gay man without a lot of noses getting bent out of joint.

I was not mistaken. The level of the dislike of gay men and the vehemence of the denial of any claim they might make for spiritual parity with their Christian "brothers" that *Corpus Christi* revealed was disheartening. Gay has never seemed less "good." Once again, we had not come a long way at all, baby.

Now I'm sounding like a homosexual.

Let me try again: If a divinity does not belong to all people, if He is not created in our image as much as we are created in His, then He is less a true divinity for all men to believe in than He is a particular religion's secular definition of what a divinity should be for the needs of its followers. Such a God is no God at all because He is exclusive to His members. He is a Roman Catholic at best and a very narrow-minded one at that.

Jesus Christ belongs to all of us because He is all of us. Unfortunately, not everyone believes that.

Very few Christians are willing to consider that their Lord and Savior was a real man with real appetites, especially sexual ones. To imagine that He was not only sexually active but a homosexual as well is gross blasphemy. And they would deny others the right to conceive of Him as such. They do not understand that a good part of our humanity is expressed *through* our sexuality and is not exclusive of it. Such a concept is as alien to them as their notion of "sin" and "evil" is to me.

In their self-defense, they tell us they hate the sin but love the sinner. Nonsense. The sinner *is* his sin and in their eyes it is an abominable one. Naturally, they tried to suppress *Corpus Christi* with threats of violence. Just as naturally, the New York theater community said no to this attempt at artistic repression and the play went on as scheduled. I have never been prouder to be a part of that community. I owe them—we all owe them—big for this one.

However, at the same time that we were all feeling so good about overcoming these forces of ignorance and prejudice, a young man in Laramie, Wyoming, by the name of Matthew Shepard was losing his life to them. Beaten senseless and tied to a split-rail fence in near-zero weather, arms akimbo in a grotesque crucifixion, he died as agonizing a death as another young man who had been tortured and nailed to a wooden cross at a desolate spot outside Jerusalem known as Golgotha some 1,998 years earlier. They died, as they lived, as brothers.

Jesus Christ did not die in vain because His disciples lived to spread His story. It is this generation's duty to make certain Matthew Shepard did not die in vain either. We forget his story at the peril of our very lives.

Maybe I should say a few words as a playwright.

The production the play received at the Manhattan Theatre Club will remain, I suspect, the definitive one. Joe Mantello is a theater poet. The appellation "director" seems too circumscribed to describe what he brings to a production. His vision for the play was met on its own high terms by the extraordinary design team and cast he assembled prior to the first day of rehearsal. Our collaboration began with *Love! Valour! Compassion!* I can only think the best is yet to come.

Corpus Christi is a passion play. The life of Joshua, a young man from south Texas, is told in the theatrical tradition of medieval morality plays. Men play all the roles. There is no suspense. There is no scenery. The purpose of the play is that we begin again the familiar dialogue with ourselves: Do I love my neighbor? Am I contributing good to the society in which I operate or nil? Do I, in fact, matter? Nothing more, nothing less. The play is more a religious ritual than a play. A play teaches us a new insight into the human condition. A ritual is an action we perform over and over because we *have* to. Otherwise, we are in danger of forgetting the meaning of that ritual, in this case that we must love one another or die. Christ died for all of our sins because He loved each and every one of us. When we do not remember His great sacrifice, we condemn ourselves to repeating its terrible consequences.

All *Corpus Christi* asks of you is to "look what they did to Him. Look what they did to Him." At the same time it asks you to look at what they did to Joshua, it asks that we look at what they did one cold October night to a young man in Wyoming as well. Jesus Christ died again when Matthew Shepard did.

Look. Remember. Weep, if you will, but learn. And don't let it happen again.

This time, I hope, I'm sounding like a human being.

Terrence McNally
New York City
November 1998

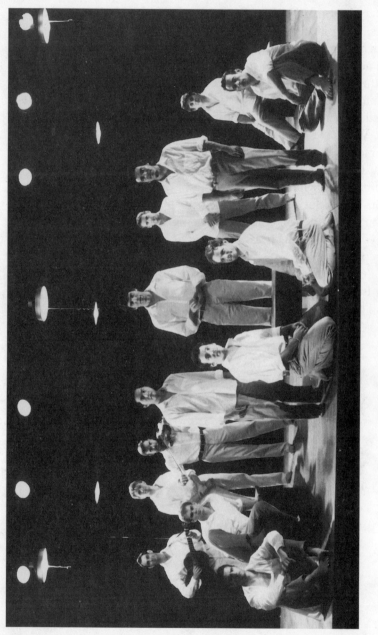

The cast of *Corpus Christi*

The Cast

The play has been written to be performed by a company of thirteen actors, all male. One actor will play the role of JOSHUA, another the role of JUDAS. The eleven other actors will play a variety of roles. The distribution of these roles will be at the discretion of the director.

The Setting

The play has been written with a bare raked stage in mind. Members of the company will sit on benches at the rear of the stage when they are not participating in a scene. Thus, an entrance is a simple stepping forward, while an exit is only a turning away and returning to the company bench. While seated, the actors observe the scene in progress and may even comment on it, either to the actors in the scene, among themselves, or to the audience.

Two design elements are important: a small pool of water and a perpetual fire, both in the floor of the stage.

Cast

Joshua
John, a writer, brother to James
James, a teacher
Peter, a young man who sells fish
Andrew, a masseur
Philip, a hustler
Bartholomew, a doctor and James's lover
Judas Iscariot, a restaurateur
Matthew, a lawyer
Thomas, an actor
James the Less, an architect
Simon, a singer
Thaddeus, a hairdresser

Corpus Christi opened on October 13, 1998, at the Manhattan Theatre Club on West Fifty-fifth Street in New York City. It was directed by Joe Mantello. The sets were by Loy Arcenas, the costumes by Jess Goldstein, and the lights by Brian MacDevitt. Sound was by David Van Tieghem and original music composed by Drew McVety. The production stage manager was James Fitzsimmons.

The company of actors who performed the play were:

Sean Dugan	James, et al.
Christopher Fitzgerald	Thomas, et al.
Michael Hall	Peter, et al.
Michael Irby	John, et al.
Ken Leung	James the Less, et al.
Josh Lucas	Judas
Matthew Mabe	Philip, et al.
Drew McVety	Matthew, et al.
Anson Mount	Joshua
Jeremy Shamos	Bartholomew, et al.
Ben Sheaffer	Simon, et al.
Troy Sostillio	Thaddeus, et al.
Greg Zola	Andrew, et al.

KOSTYA (*looking round the stage*) There's a theatre for you! Just a curtain, two wings, and then open space. Not a bit of scenery. A view straight onto the lake and the far horizon. We'll raise the curtain at half past eight, exactly, when the moon rises.

Anton Chekhov, *The Seagull*, Act One

The house lights are still up as the ACTORS *begin to drift on stage. They are wearing street clothes. They may either talk among themselves, greet people in the audience, or quietly prepare for the performance. Some of them will check the prop tables, which are visible stage right and left. The mood is informal, lightly bantering, loving even.*

The play itself "begins" when from offstage we hear the three loud, deliberate knocks of a wooden staff forcefully striking the stage floor. At once the ACTORS *are silent and gather in a more formal grouping.*

Again, the three knocks from offstage.

One of the ACTORS *steps forward.*

Actor We are going to tell you an old and familiar story. One you've all heard over and over, again and again. One you believe or one you don't. There's no suspense and fewer surprises. You all know how it turns out. But it's a story that bears repeating. Some say it can't be told enough. The playwright asks your indulgence, as do we, the actors. There are no tricks up our sleeves. No malice in our hearts. We're glad you're here.

The house lights are lowered. One of the ACTORS *begins to sing (a capella) "Were You There When They Crucified My Lord?" The other* ACTORS *join in as they begin to undress and change into the "uniform" of the play: white shirt, khaki trousers, and bare feet.*

The ACTOR *playing* JOHN *cups his hands together while the actor playing* PETER *fills them with water from a pitcher. One by one, the other actors will pass in front of the actor playing* JOHN, *who raises his cupped hands over them and lets the water run down their bared heads.*

John I bless you, (full name of the actor playing ANDREW). I baptize you and recognize your divinity as a human being. I adore you, (first name of the actor playing ANDREW). I christen you Andrew.

Andrew Andrew's hands were his livelihood. He was a masseur. He didn't say much when he worked. He didn't figure he had to. Already I've said more. If he liked you, you knew it. If he didn't like you, you really knew it. And if he loved you! Bliss. Andrew loved Joshua. That was our name for Him. He loved Joshua a lot.

ANDREW *turns away and continues to dress as the actor playing* JAMES *steps forward and kneels before the actor playing* JOHN. *This same ritual will continue until all eleven other actors are baptized. After he is so blessed and has introduced himself, each actor will finish changing into his plain white shirt and crisp pair of khakis while remaining barefoot.*

Now JOHN *baptizes the actor playing* JAMES.

John I bless you, (full name of the actor playing JAMES). I baptize you and recognize your divinity as a human being. I adore you, (first name of the actor). I christen you James.

James I'm a teacher. High school. It's a tough age. I teach history, world history. They hate it. I don't care. I love what I do. What happened and why. How we learn from it or we don't. Cool. Very cool. I love my sandwich and apple in a brown paper bag. I love chalk and blackboards and erasers and maps you pull down of the Roman Empire. I can see where I am on it. This little dot, Corpus Christi, and I'm there. I love that.

JAMES *turns away as the actor playing* BARTHOLOMEW *steps forward.*

John I bless you, (full name of the actor playing BARTHOLOMEW). I baptize you and recognize your divinity as a human being. I adore you, (first name of the actor). I christen you Bartholomew.

Bartholomew I hope that's not the same water we used the last performance. Laugh, but Bartholomew was a doctor. That's exactly the kind of thing he'd be worried about. We have to heal men's bodies before we can heal their souls. Joshua didn't always understand that. "Believe," He'd say, "believe and be well." I'd be right behind Him saying, "Believe and take two of these and call me in the morning."

John I bless you, (full name of the actor playing SIMON). I baptize you and recognize your divinity as a human being. I adore you, (first name of the actor playing SIMON). I christen you Simon.

Simon Thank you. I love being Simon. Simon was a singer. Well, among other things he was a singer. First and foremost he was a disciple, a follower of Joshua. I don't know why following has such a bad name. With the right leader, with the right guys, it can be wonderful. All my life I wanted to belong to something and here I was, right smack in the middle. I hope you're as fortunate. I know this much: Before I had to sing to be happy. Now I sing because I am happy. I'm singing all the time.

John I bless you, (full name of the actor playing MATTHEW). I baptize you and recognize your divinity as a human being. I adore you, (first name of the actor playing MATTHEW). I christen you Matthew.

Matthew Matthew was a lawyer, a brilliant one. The kind they write novels about. He had it all: a corner office, a drop-dead apartment, a good car, a house at the beach. He was made a full partner at thirty-one. Are you impressed? He was. We had a lot to get over. I believe it's called attitude. The first time I met Joshua I didn't like Him. I'd worked very hard to get this much of a piece of the pie—a lot of us had—(my father delivered mail!) and here He was saying I had to give it all away. It pissed me off. He still does sometimes but hey, I'm learning to be a team player, you know? It's not easy. I had a corner office.

John I bless you, (full name of the actor playing THOMAS). I baptize you and recognize your divinity as a human being. I adore you, (first name of the actor playing THOMAS). I christen you Thomas.

Thomas I'm an actor. I mean Thomas is an actor. I'm an actor, too, of course, but you know that or you wouldn't be paying good money or even no money to sit there and listen to me tell you I'm someone else, in this case the ever popular and appealing Thomas. It's called the willing suspension of disbelief—or in certain cases the *un*willing suspension of disbelief. I've seen audiences fight a play for an entire performance. At the end of the evening, they're exhausted. So are we. I bet even the ushers and the stagehands are feeling the fatigue. Why do that to yourself? Or us? We want to take you someplace beautiful, someplace thrilling, someplace maybe you've never been before. Come with us. At least meet us halfway. I think you'll like Thomas. I know I do. We're both twenty-five. We never get the girl. Or the guy. We're both character actors, which is short for short and not looking like some of these other bimbos. I'm going to play the shit out of this part.

John I bless you, (full name of the actor playing JAMES THE LESS). I baptize you and recognize your divinity as a human being. I adore you, (first name of the actor playing JAMES THE LESS). I christen you James the Less.

James the Less Hell of a name to stick someone with but it was in fact what Joshua called me when it turned out He already had a James. I didn't take it personally, He lied. This James, James the Less, was an architect. He had a profound sense of order, a subtle intuition for volume, almost a child's delight in the play of light and shadow and a passionate commitment to function. What he designed had to work, it had to do something. Otherwise, why make it? I designed the Roman cross, I'm ashamed to say. At the time, I thought nothing of it. The perfect killing machine, they called it. An idiot could have thought of it. If you do this to someone (*he holds his arms out*)—after a while their lungs implode and they suffocate. I hate the Romans.

John I bless you, (full name of the actor playing THADDEUS). I baptize you and recognize your divinity as a human being. I adore you, (first name of the actor playing THADDEUS). I christen you Thaddeus.

Thaddeus Thaddeus was a hairdresser. Does anybody have a problem with that? Good.

John I bless you, (full name of the actor playing PHILIP). I baptize you and recognize your divinity as a human being. I adore you, (first name of the actor playing PHILIP). I christen you Philip.

Philip They don't know much about me. I like that. This much is certain: He was probably Greek. His father was an apothecary. He was in his early thirties when he met Joshua and the others. They have no idea how old he was when he died or how. And that's all, folks. They don't know anything else about him. He's not one of those people who leave a record. I like being Philip. I can be anyone I want to be. Except Him. I could never be Him.

Matthew You didn't tell them you were a hustler.

Philip It must have slipped my mind.

Simon Give it a rest, Matthew.

The Actor Playing Peter Excuse me, do you think we could do me now?

John I'm sorry, of course. I bless you, (full name of the actor playing SIMON PETER).

The Actor Playing Peter That's better already.

John I baptize you and recognize your divinity as a human being. I adore you, (first name of the actor playing SIMON PETER). I christen you Peter.

Peter Peter, Simon Peter is probably the most familiar of us to you. Well, after Joshua, of course. And I suppose Judas Iscariot. And John the Baptist, I guess. Let me start again. Peter, Simon Peter is probably the fourth most familiar of us to you. He was a fisherman. Nothing made him happier than to come home with his nets bulging with fish he'd pulled from the sea with his own two hands. Tuna, red snapper, cod. The occasional eel. He loved that flopping sound they made on his deck. There'd be good eating tonight. The first time I saw Joshua it took my breath away. I forgot all about my fish. Half of them flopped right back into the sea. I didn't care.

TWO ACTORS remain. The others have formed a half circle around them.

John One of you must be Him.

The Actor Playing Joshua Is it I?

The Actor Playing Judas Is it I?

John You know who it is. Accept it.

ONE of the TWO ACTORS stands up and comes forward.

The Actor Playing Joshua It is I.

John I bless you, (full name of the actor playing JOSHUA). I baptize you and recognize your divinity as a human being. I love you, (first name of the actor playing JOSHUA). I christen you Jesus, son of Mary and Joseph, son of God, son of man.

The ACTOR *howls as if scalded as the water is poured over him.*

John I christen you Joshua.

The ACTOR *has stopped howling.*

I've been waiting for You.

Thaddeus We all have.

THADDEUS *takes* JOHN's *place as* THE ACTOR PLAYING JOHN *kneels while* JOSHUA *blesses and baptizes him,* THADDEUS *helping with the pitcher of water.*

Joshua I bless you, (full name of the actor playing JOHN). I baptize you and recognize your divinity as a human being. I adore you, (first name of the actor playing JOHN). I christen you John, my cousin.

THADDEUS *and* MATTHEW *bring* JOSHUA *and* JOHN *their white shirts and khakis. They begin to dress.*

John I was lucky. I was born with faith. I knew You would come.

Joshua How did you know it was Me when even I didn't?

John There was a halo around Your head, coz.

Joshua Be serious!

John I am. You're the only one who didn't see it. Are we all here then?

One ACTOR *has remained alone and apart from the others.*

The Actor Playing Judas What about me?

Joshua Come.

JOSHUA motions the actor forward. He kneels before JOSHUA for his blessing and baptism but he does not bow his head. Instead he looks right at JOSHUA.

Judas So here we are again.

Joshua I bless you, (full name of the actor playing JUDAS). I baptize you and recognize your divinity as a human being.

The ACTOR shudders as the water is poured over him.

I adore you, (first name of the actor playing JUDAS). I christen you Judas.

The ACTOR stops shuddering and looks up at JOSHUA.

Joshua I did love you, you know.

Judas Not the way I wanted.

The other ACTORS line the stage apron, impatient to begin.

Judas Judas Iscariot, Scorpio. November sixth. You figure the year. I'm smart. I like to read. I like music. Good music. I like the theater. Good theater. I like some sports. I like violence. I take good care of myself. Weak bodies disgust me. I've got a big dick.

There are razzes from the ranks.

It's important. It's important to me. Everybody is going to tell the truth about himself this time! Even Joshua.

Joshua Especially Joshua.

James Get on with it, Judas.

Judas No one has ever told this story right. Even when they get the facts right, the feeling is wrong. One and one are two. So what? What does that tell you about anything? This is what matters.

JUDAS hits his right hand into his chest.

The only thing. Nothing else.

More razzes. JUDAS continues over them.

People can't stand the truth. They want their Joshua, seen through their eyes, told through their lies. Truth is brutal. It scalds, it stings.

JUDAS is being shouted down by the OTHERS. SIMON and PHILIP have gone to the prop table and picked up a large basket filled with folded slips of paper. They will pass in front of the OTHERS, who will draw five or six slips apiece. On these folded slips of paper are written the names of the other "roles" they will play in the story that follows.

Simon We need a cast of thousands to tell this story: men, women, children.

James the Less None of us knows who he's going to be.

Philip It's the luck of the draw.

Bartholomew A Roman centurion.

Thaddeus I'll trade you for Peggy Powell.

Thomas Lazarus! Finally! Something I can get my teeth into.

James Much scenery will be chewed at this performance!

Thomas It's a very emotional story. So I'm not a minimalist.

John Does everybody know who they are? All right, props!

One by one various props are displayed to the audience and then returned to their place on the prop tables or in the wings.

Andrew Nails. More like small spikes actually. Jesus, look at these things!

Philip A hammer to drive the nails.

John Thirty pieces of silver and a noose.

Thomas A loaf of bread.

Thaddeus Rope. For He was bound to a pillar and scourged.

James the Less The scourge.

Matthew A crown of thorns.

Simon His mother's Grand Ole Opry souvenir ashtray.

Peter I'll take that, thank you.

Thomas A fish.

    THOMAS *holds up a fresh fish.*

Pee-eew!

Bartholomew Vinegar.

Andrew A sponge.

Thaddeus The spear that pierced His side to end His dreadful suffering.

Peter The chalice.

Simon His little dog, Nebuchadnezzar.

    The dog is a stuffed animal on wheels that is easily pulled behind you.

James the Less (*to us*) I bet you didn't know about the little dog.

Matthew (*the same*) Every kid has a dog.

Peter A pair of blue suede shoes.

Simon A pink suede belt.

James A high school varsity letter.

Thomas Cool.

Matthew For what sport?

Joshua Speech and drama.

Matthew Not cool. A picture of James Dean.

Joshua Let them see it.

MATTHEW gives the picture to someone in the first row.

Matthew Pass it around, will you? Thanks.

Peter A pack of Lucky Strike cigarettes, their stubs carefully snuffed out in a Maxwell House coffee can kept hidden under His bed along with the picture of James Dean.

James A copy of the Old Testament. The new one hasn't been written yet.

Bartholomew His diary. No one knew He kept one.

JUDAS is sitting on one of the benches, staying apart from the others.

Judas I did.

Bartholomew Anyway, it was lost. Imagine if it hadn't been.

James We wouldn't be doing this.

Joshua The cross? What about the cross?

John They're making it.

JOHN nods offstage.

Hear them?

We can hear the sound of hammering from offstage.

Joshua No.

John That's because You don't want to hear them. Are we ready then? Scene One. The nativity.

JOHN is a great stage manager. When he claps his hands, people jump to it. The stage is a swirl of activity as the ACTORS set up for the next scene.

The ACTORS *not in the scene sit on the benches at the rear of the stage and watch. They may occasionally comment on the scene that follows. They definitely supply appropriate sound effects.*

Actors "Away in a manger
No crib for his bed

O little town of Bethlehem
How still we see thee lie

Jingle bells, jingle bells
Jingle all the way"

A TV is blaring. A football game is in progress.

A MOTEL MANAGER *is showing a vacant room to* PETER/MARY, *mother of* JOSHUA, *whose abdomen bulges as if pregnant.*

Bartholomew/Motel Manager It's a big football weekend. This is the best we have. Take it or leave it, lady.

Peter/Mary It's fine.

Motel Manager Where's your uh husband?

Mary Unloading the car.

Motel Manager How soon are you going to, you know, pop?

Mary I think right now.

MARY *gives birth and takes a doll out from under her skirt.*

Motel Manager Jesus Christ. What is it?

Mary A boy.

Motel Manager That's good. I like boys. Boys are best. The ice machine is outside to your left. (*At a cheer from the TV*) They scored again! I fucking don't believe it. (*To* MARY, *who has begun to nurse*) Hey, you're not going to try anything funny with that kid. You know, stuff him down the crapper or something. Don't laugh. It wouldn't be the first. That's the last fucking thing I need this weekend: an infantesticide

12

Michael Hall as Mary

... (*He has trouble with such a long word*) ... that's what they call 'em!

MOTEL MANGER goes. One of the ACTORS begins to play "Ave Maria" on the violin. If no one in the cast can play "Ave Maria" on the violin, one of them should pantomime it to recorded music. The ACTOR will enter the playing area of the motel scene but be invisible to the participants.

MARY cradles a doll in his arm as JOSHUA makes gurgling, crying "baby" sounds appropriate for a newborn infant.

Mary Ssssh, ssshh, it's all right. Mommy's here.

Sung.

"Rockabye, baby, up a ... something, something tree.
Lullaby and good night.
Rockaby your baby with a Dixie melody."

Joshua I was so cute! Look at me! Where did all that blond hair come from?

We hear sounds of a couple making wild, uninhibited love in the room next door.

Mary Such a beautiful child He is. Perfect limbs. Perfect features.

Joshua And you were so pretty! Look how pretty My mom was, everyone. Like someone in the movies!

Woman Next Door/James Fuck me, fuck me, fuck me.

Man Next Door/Andrew That's what I'm doing, you damn woman. I'm fucking you, I'm fucking you, I'm fucking you.

PHILIP *gets up from his place on the bench and comes into the motel room.* HE IS JOSHUA'S *father,* JOSEPH.

Philip/Joseph Sounds like somebody's having some fun next door. Is that? So soon? It's big. I didn't think it would be so big. Can I hold it? Thank you. It's a boy. Hey, little fella. You gonna grow up and be an All-American halfback? (*To* MARY) You look so beautiful, Mother. Radiant.

Joshua How they must have loved each other!

Joseph This isn't easy for me to say, Mare, but I'm going to love Him like He's my own, even if He's not.

Joshua My father said that. My father loved me!

Mary He's not anyone else's. I swear on my life. I'm a virgin, Joe.

Joseph No one knows that more than I do.

Mary I don't know what's going on here any more than you do.

Joseph What are we gonna tell people when I take you back home?

Mary It's none of their damn business. And I'm not saying he's adopted!

Joseph What are we gonna call Him?

Mary I told you. Jesus.

Joseph I told you no. This is Texas. It sounds like a Mexican.

Mary I love Him so much already. Don't judge us too harshly, son.

> SIMON, THADDEUS, *and* THOMAS *begin singing:*
> *"We three kings of Orient are*
> *Bearing gifts we travel afar."*

Oh, listen, they're singing! I love Christmas.

The THREE *enter the room together.*

Simon/Room Service #1 Room service!

Joseph We didn't order.

Room Service #1 It's on the house. We heard something very special was happening in room thirty-seven tonight.

Joseph Something very special has.

Thaddeus/Room Service #2 I hope you like Cuban cigars, Dad. Congratulations.

Joseph Why thank you kindly.

Thomas/Room Service #3 I know you didn't order this but every boy wants a Flexible Flyer sled when he grows up.

Joseph We're from south Texas, mister. It hasn't snowed in Corpus Christi since the last time Hell froze over, which is never, if you catch my drift.

Joshua Thank you anyway.

It begins to snow.

Look, everybody!

Joseph Jesus Christ, Mary!

Mary It's a miracle.

Joshua It's not a miracle. It's snow.

Thomas/Room Service #3 What's Your name, little tiger?

Joshua They haven't given Me one yet.

Room Service #3 You're going to save the world no matter what they call You. Beowulf, Charlemagne, Lucille Ball. What's in a name? It's who You are, what You do that matters.

Joshua Thank you, sir.

Room Service #1 Are you the mother? We have tidings for the mother, too.

Joseph Doesn't she look wonderful for a woman who's just given birth to a very large child, gentlemen?

Room Service #1 Hail, Mary, full of grace. The Lord is with thee.

Mary Well, I don't know about that but thank you kindly.

Room Service #2 Blessed is the fruit of thy womb, Jesus.

Mary We decided to call him Joshua actually.

Room Service #1 We bear you tidings: This is the child the world has waited for.

Room Service #2 He will die for our sins: mine and yours.

Room Service #3 His love for the world will redeem us all.

Mary So you're telling me He's a special child?

Room Service #1 We're telling you this child is the son of God.

Mary Hell, every mother feels that way.

Room Service #1 Cherish and love Him.

Mary What does it look like I'm doing? You have some kid chewing on your tits and see how you like it. And I don't need a bunch a strangers telling me I don't know how to raise my own child.

Joseph She's just a little testy.

Mary I'm not testy, I'm sore. I wish everybody would get out of here.

Joseph We got a long drive tomorrow. Thanks for the presents and the good wishes, gentlemen. Happy holidays.

THOMAS, THADDEUS, *and* SIMON *return to the bench, singing "We Three Kings of Orient Are" as they go.*

Joseph Hey, it's Christmas. Are we gonna drink us a couple o' tequila sunrises and do us a little jukin' or what? Elvis has a new hit out.

Mary What if my child needs me?

Joseph I'll tell you who needs you: I do. Now, I'll give you fifteen seconds, Mare. Not thirty. Not twenty. Fifteen. You got that?

Mary Got it. (Die.)

JOSEPH *goes back to the bench.*

You look like You're trying to say something. That's all I need: a kid who starts talking early, like I don't have enough of a headache. Who are You? Where did You come from? I know You're not really mine.

Joshua Sshh, sshh, you don't have to talk. Just hold Me.

Joseph Mary!

Mary If You're the son of God, what does that make me?

Joshua The mother of the son of God.

Mary I don't know if I can do this.

Joshua Sure you can. It's easy. You're doing great.

Joseph Goddamnit, Mary!

Troy Sostillio, Christopher Fitzgerald, and and Ben Sheaffer as the Three Wise Men

Joshua Leave us alone!

Joseph One!

Mary So little!

Joshua I'm sorry. I'll grow. I promise.

Joseph Two!

Mary So unprotected!

Joshua That's okay. I have you.

Joseph Three!

Joshua Don't go.

Mary I'm sorry. He's calling me.

Joseph Goddamnit it all to hell!

Mary Coming!

MARY goes. JOSHUA stands looking down at the doll and makes baby sounds again.

And now we hear the sounds of a terrible fight coming from the room on the other side of JOSHUA's.

Angry Man/John You stupid piece of shit. You fucking cow.

Frightened Woman/Matthew I'm sorry. Just don't hit me again.

Angry Man/John Just don't (*sounds of a hit*) you again? Is that what you said? Just don't fucking (*sounds of a hit*) hit you again? Is that what you (*sounds of a hit, sounds of a hit, sounds of a hit*) fucking said to me?

Silence. We hear only JOSHUA's baby sounds.

Angry Man Now what? You just gonna lie there like that? Fuck this shit.

Sounds of a door slamming.

James the Less/God Joshua. Joshua. Joshua. This is the Lord God, Your father. Stop crying and be a man. Much has been given to You because much is expected of You. Men are cruel. They are not happy. They sicken and die and turn away from love. I want You to show them there is another way. The way of love and generosity and self-peace. You will comfort a woman who lies battered in a motel room next to Yours. You will forgive the man who left her there. You will teach a couple in another motel room that there is more to love than—

Woman Next Door/James Fuck me, fuck me, fuck me!

God —but You will allow them that—

Man Next Door/Bartholemew I'm fucking you, I'm fucking you, I'm fucking you!

God —has its pleasures, too. You will work miracles. You will demonstrate patience and practice inexorable determination. When You are much too young You will die a terrible death at the very hands of those I gave You to. Before then You will know suffering but You will also know laughter and friendship and the joy of skinny-dipping on a warm summer's day and the pleasure of a fine meal of roast lamb and fresh-baked bread washed down with a hearty red wine. Your name will still be spoken all the years after Your birth.

Joshua You said I will suffer?

God Terribly. But You will know great joy as well.

Joshua Why must I suffer?

God Why not?

Joshua Why Me?

God Why not You?

> GOD *whispers something in* JOSHUA's *ear.*

Joshua What? I couldn't hear You.

God All men are divine.

Joshua Why are You whispering?

God That is the secret You will teach them.

Joshua What if I don't want to share this secret with My fellow men?

God You won't be able to keep it.

Joshua What if I don't believe it Myself?

God No more questions. I'm gone, Joshua.

Joshua What do You mean, You're gone? You can't be gone. You're supposed to be everywhere all the time.

God That is a very big misunderstanding.

BARTHOLOMEW crosses to JOSHUA.

Bartholomew Give Him to me.

BARTHOLOMEW takes the doll.

Joshua What for?

Bartholomew The circumcision.

Thomas Could we just skip this scene?

Bartholomew Everybody's so squeamish.

Matthew/Priest Why aren't You playing football?

Joshua I don't want to.

Priest What kind of answer is that, boy? Sure You do! Every boy in Corpus Christi plays football.

The other ACTORS have begun to toss footballs back and forth, having fun.

How old are You?

Joshua Thirteen.

Priest Thirteen? You're small for Your age. I thought You were ten. (*Calling to another boy*) How old would you say this one looks?

Boy Nine. He's in the wrong school!

Priest They ought to get You some of them hormone shots. Let me see You throw a football.

JOSHUA throws the ball.

That's not how You throw a football. This is how You throw a football. Are You gonna cry on me?

Joshua No, sir.

Priest You like scouts?

Joshua Yes, sir.

Priest Good, we'll make a football player out of You. You like pussy? Pussy is girls. You like girls?

Joshua Yes, sir.

This time JOSHUA *throws the ball with startling speed and accuracy, catching the* PRIEST *off guard. He throws it back to* JOSHUA. *The football goes back and forth with increasing hostility. Again the other boys stop to watch.*

Priest You got a girlfriend?

Joshua No, sir.

Priest Well then maybe You don't like girls.

Joshua Yes, sir.

Priest You gonna say yes, sir, no, sir to every cotton-picking thing I say?

Joshua I'm sorry, sir.

Priest Sir-ring somebody like that don't sound polite. It sounds more like sass and nobody likes to be sassed. Especially an overworked, underpaid Roman Catholic priest who has to be a goddamn scoutmaster after school. Don't You think I have better things to do with my time than try to teach You how to throw a football?

Joshua Ow. You're hurting Me.

Priest Well ain't that a Goddamn shame.

Sister Joseph Leave the child alone, Father McMullen. He's late for play practice.

Priest Of course, Sister Joseph. We were just playing. See why we never get married, Josh? So some woman can't tell us what to do the rest of our life.

PRIEST goes.

22

Sister Joseph There goes a man who doesn't like who he is. Are You all right?

Joshua Yes, sister.

SISTER *goes to a piano.* JOSHUA *stands center stage.*

Sister Joseph I hope you've been working on Your number. We open in two weeks. Now set the scene for Yourself. You're alone on a beautiful beach. You're in love. Have You ever been in love, Joshua?

Joshua No, ma'am.

Sister Joseph Well, as I used to say before I took my holy vows, we'll just have to fake it.

SISTER JOSEPH *plays an elaborate flourish.*

And . . .

Joshua (*singing*)	**Sister Joseph** (*interjecting*)
"I'm as corny as Kansas in August.	Let loose, Joshua. No matter what else You do, learn to
I'm as normal as blueberry pie.	let loose.
No more the smart little girl with no heart	
I have found me a wonderful guy."	

Sister Joseph Who are You saving it for anyway? Seven, eight . . .

Joshua (*resumes singing*)	**Sister Joseph** (*interjecting*)
"I'm as corny as Kansas in August	
High as the flag on the fourth of July	There you go!
If you'll excuse the expression I use	
I'm in love	

Sister Joseph "I'm in love"

Joshua "I'm in love"

Sister Joseph "I'm in love"

Joshua and Sister Joseph "I'm in love with a wonderful guy."

Mary You through with Him, sister?

Sister Joseph Show your mother what we've been doing, Joshua.

Mary I saw enough, thank you. Not quite my cup of tea. I'm driving Him to his ballroom dance class. They're teaching Him to hold a woman proper. I figure that's a little out of your milieu, sister.

Sister Joseph Ballroom dance class? They grow up so fast. He's a very special child.

Mary I've been hearing that all His life. I'm still waiting.

Joshua Good-bye, sister. I'll remember what you said.

Mary What did she say?

Joshua Nothing.

Mary You start listening to nuns, You're going to get Yourself entirely screwed up.

> MARY *holds up a 45-rpm record. The violin music gets much livelier.*

Now whose little sixth grader is ready to rock and roll with His ol' mama!

> JOSHUA *tries to dance with* MARY.

Mary No, darlin', put Your hands around me this way. The man leads the woman. Just listen to the music. It'll tell You what to do. I give up.

Joshua Do you ever hear hammering?

Mary Your father's a carpenter. Of course I hear hammering. What's the matter with You?

Joshua I'm sorry.

Mary You're not much of a dancer either. All those lessons!

Joshua No, ma'am.

Mary And I'm a woman who loves to dance.

Joshua Yes, ma'am.

Mary I told Your father: no wonder I go out nights. I'm just looking for someone who wants to dance with me. Hell, I even tried to turn You into a little Gene Kelly.

Joshua Don't cry, ma'am.

Mary I'm not crying. Why should I cry? And don't start that ma'am business with me, Joshua. We're both too old for it.

Joshua I'm seventeen. I just look young for My age. So do you. You're still so beautiful.

Mary You're a sweet boy, Joshua. Too bad You're not a dancer. We could have had some fun.

PHILIP/MRS. MCELROY has begun to set up a chess board.

Joshua There's Mrs. McElroy. I gotta go.

Mary I'm not through with You.

But JOSHUA has already joined MRS. MCELROY.

Joshua I memorized another Shakespeare sonnet, Mrs. McElroy. "When to the—"

James/Mrs. McElroy Slow down, Joshua, not so fast!

The fiddler begins to play "The Meditation" from Massenet's opera Thais.

Mary What are you teaching Him at that public high school of yours, Mrs. McElroy?

Joshua She's teaching Me that this town is the armpit of Western civilization.

Mrs. McElroy Joshua!

Joshua "When to the sessions of sweet silent thought."

Mary 'Cause you're not teaching Him to dance.

Joshua "I summon up remembrance of thing past."

Mary You're not teaching Him to love and respect His own mother. I've got my eye on you. I know what you're doing.

She goes back to the bench and sits.

Mrs. McElroy You're going to get me into trouble with Your folks.

They begin to play chess.

Joshua My mother doesn't like Me, Mrs. McElroy, and My father is never around.

Mrs. McElroy It's hard, I know. When I was Your age I . . .

Joshua What? Tell Me!

Mrs. McElroy I've always found consolation in the masterpieces of English literature, especially the Romantic poets.

Joshua What do you have to be consoled about? I'll console you.

Mrs. McElroy Your move, Joshua.

Joshua What's that music? It's pretty.

Mrs. McElroy This particular selection is known as "The Meditation" from *Thais*, a French opera by one Jules Massenet.

Joshua Jules Massenet.

Mrs. McElroy The eponymous heroine sits looking at her reflection in a mirror, meditating that her beauty, like all else, it, too, shall fade.

Joshua I think you're beautiful.

As the ACTOR *who plays the fiddle rips into a lively dance tune, the other* ACTORS *erupt from the benches in a noisy phalanx of rootin', tootin'* TEENAGERS. JOSHUA *continues with* MRS. MCELROY. *Only* JUDAS *remains alone on the bench, watching the others.*

Matthew The theme for this year's senior prom is "A Night in Nineveh."

Simon Who says?

Matthew I did. Peggy Powell, you're in charge of decorations.

Bartholomew/Peggy Powell I need volunteers.

Peter Me!

Simon Me!

John Me, Peggy!

Peggy I want Joshua.

Joshua Sure, Peggy. Excuse me, Mrs. McElroy.

Mrs. McElroy (*after him*) Sonnet Sixty-four next time, my favorite. "The expense of spirit."

Joshua (*going*) "In a waste of shame." I already know it.

JOSHUA *has joined* PEGGY.

Peggy Are You in love with Mrs. McElroy?

Joshua Don't be ridiculous, Peggy. She's an old woman. She's like thirty and she has two children.

Peggy You act like You're in love with her.

Anson Mount as Joshua and Jeremy Shamos as Peggy Powell

Joshua Gross Me out, why don't you! She understands Me. My parents don't. Sometimes I don't think they're really My parents.

Peggy Every teenager feels like that. So who are You going to ask to the prom?

Joshua I don't know. Who are you going with?

Peggy Dub Taylor and Spider Sloan and Billy Brown all asked me but I sort of told them all no. I sort of told them I was hoping someone else would ask me and if he didn't then maybe I'd go with Billy Brown but I would never go with Dub or Spider.

James the Less/Billy Brown He stares at me all the time.

John/Dub Taylor You mean in the shower.

Billy Brown I don't just mean in the shower. I mean in home room, I mean in chemistry, I mean in civics.

Peter/Spider Sloan He's in love with you, Billy.

Billy Brown Shut up, Spider.

Dub Taylor Okay, so you're in love with Him.

Billy Brown You, too, Dub.

PETER, SIMON, *and* MATTHEW *snap towels at each other, wrestle, etc.*

Peggy They're coarse, uncouth rednecks. Billy's a little better but not much. So who do You want to ask as opposed to probably will because You think You should who or just because You're pretty sure she'll say yes who?

Joshua Patricia Rudd.

Thomas/Patricia I'd love to, Joshua.

Peggy She's practically the ugliest girl in the whole school.

Patricia Nuts to you, Peggy! Have another abortion nobody's supposed to know about!

Andrew/Bert Moody Welcome to Pontius Pilate High senior class prom. For those of you who have been living under a rock for the past four years, I am your on-his-way-to-med-school-like-a-rocket senior class president, Bert Moody. I want to thank Peggy and Joshua for the splendid decorations.

Simon Love that feminine touch, Joshua.

Patricia Don't listen to them, Josh.

Bert I have the winners of the favorites contest. Please step up to the bandstand as your name is called. Most Beautiful and Most Handsome.

BERT *opens an envelope.*

Patricia (So what else is new?) Peggy Powell and Beau Hunter.

Bert For the fourth year in a row, the winners are Peggy Powell and Beau Hunter.

Beau I just want to say: blinding good looks aren't everything.

Bert Very funny, Beau, very funny. We understand you'll be majoring in stand-up comedy at Texas Tech.

Peggy I believe Beau is speaking about inner beauty.

Simon He has to. Did you ever see the size of his dick!

James/Mrs. McElroy (*Ready to report names*) Who said that? Who said that?

Bert Most Popular. Darlene Taylor and Bert Moody. Bert Moody, oh my God, that's me! Why thank you. Where's Darlene?

Peter She's having her period.

Mrs. McElroy Who is saying these things? They are headed straight to Mr. Franklin's office.

Peter Fuck Mr. Franklin.

Bert Most Likely to Take It Up the Hershey Highway. Joshua. I don't know how this got in here. That wasn't funny. I'm sorry, Joshua. Most Likely to Succeed. Mary Swanson and Stanford Walsh.

> *The band strikes up "Unchained Melody."* SIMON *sings while all the other* ACTORS *dance.* PATRICIA *and* JOSHUA *dance together downstage.*

Patricia What they did was stupid and cruel and why I am going to write the president of the United States telling him that if there is any place in this country where nuclear bomb testing should be allowed, it's Corpus Christi, Texas. Ow!

Joshua I'm sorry.

Thaddeus May I cut in?

Patricia I don't know.

Joshua That's okay.

JOSHUA *leaves them to dance together.*

Thaddeus Oh, God.

Patricia What's wrong?

Thaddeus I'm getting a hard-on.

THADDEUS *whirls* PATRICIA *into the swirl of the other dancers. Everyone is dancing now but* JOSHUA *and* JUDAS.

JOSHUA *moves away from them and takes out a pack of Lucky Strikes and lights one. He is outside the gym where the dance is being held now.*

Simon "I need your love
I need your love
God speed your love."

God This is My beloved son in whom I take great delight.

Joshua Who said that? Why won't you leave Me alone?

Simon "To . . . me . . . Bop, shoo wa do wop . . . Bop, shoo wa do wop."

JAMES THE LESS, JOHN, *and* PETER *appear. They will take a leak, smoke, check their hair, etc.*

John/Dub Taylor If you can't fuck her tonight, you're never gonna fuck her.

Peter/Spider Sloan Look who's talking!

James the Less/Billy Brown You'd be the only guy in Pontius Pilate High who hasn't fucked her.

He sees JOSHUA.

Well almost the only guy in Pontius Pilate High who hasn't fucked her. You haven't fucked Penny Porter, have you, Joshua?

Peter/Spider Ssshhh! Can't you see He's trying to take a leak. The man can't take a leak with you yakking at him. (*Standing next to* JOSHUA, *shoulder to shoulder*) Can he?

Billy That's the God's honest truth. (*On the other side of* JOSHUA *now*): But you know what's worse than a guy yakking at you while you're trying to piss? It's a guy looking at your dick while you're trying to piss. I hate it when a guy does that. I hate it a lot.

John What do you do to someone like that, Billy?

Billy Well the last guy who did that to me I beat the shit out of him and then I stuck his head in the toilet until he said he wasn't gonna look at anybody's dick while they were trying to take a piss ever again in his whole fucked-up fairy queer life.

Dub I guess that was telling him.

Billy I guess it was. What do You say to that, Joshua?

Spider He can't say anything, Billy.

Billy Why not?

Spider He's too busy looking at your dick.

BILLY and DUB try to duck JOSHUA's head in the urinal, yelling "Flush it, flush it."

Judas Leave Him alone.

Billy We were just fooling around.

Dub We didn't mean anything. Honest.

Spider Tell him. We were just. . . . Okay, okay. We're gone.

They are gone.

Joshua Thank you.

Judas Thank you? I save Your life and that's all I get? Thank you?

Joshua I don't think they were actually going to kill Me.

Judas You would have wished they had. I'm Judas.

Joshua I'm Joshua.

Judas I know. I've seen You. You don't have many friends. That's okay, I'll be your friend. You talk to Yourself. "This is My son in whom I take much delight." I've heard You. You can talk to me now.

Joshua That wasn't Me.

Judas Nobody here but us chickens. It must have been somebody.

Joshua What are you staring at?

Judas You. Does it bother You?

Joshua No. I can stare right back.

Judas First one who looks away has to buy a six-pack, okay?

Joshua Okay. I always win this game.

Judas So do I.

Joshua Are we playing?

Judas We're playing.

Joshua Who'd you come with?

Judas No one.

Joshua How come?

Judas I don't like girls. What about You?

Joshua What do you mean, what about Me?

Judas You like girls?

Joshua Yes, I like girls.

Judas Just asking, Joshua.

Joshua I like boys, too. I like people.

Judas You're lucky. I don't.

Joshua Don't what?

Judas Like people. You ever play the other side of "Heartbreak Hotel"?

    JOSHUA *shakes his head.*

You never turned it over?

    JOSHUA *shakes his head.*

That's the difference between us. Curiosity.

Joshua I'm curious.

Judas I bet you are. So who's Your favorite movie star?

Joshua Marilyn Monroe.

Judas She can't act.

Joshua I don't care. I like her. She's pretty. What about James Dean?

Judas He can't act either. I'd like to do it with him though.

Joshua I beg your pardon?

Judas I'd like to do it with him. You looked away. I win. What's my prize?

Joshua You said a six-pack.

Judas I got a better idea.

He kisses JOSHUA *on the lips.* PATRICIA *enters.*

Patricia There You are. I looked.

Judas Hello.

Joshua This is Judas. This is Patricia.

Patricia I'll be on the dance floor.

PATRICIA *goes.*

Joshua We shouldn't have done that.

Judas Who says? Open your mouth next time somebody kisses You.

Bert Moody Last dance! Find the girl you came with for the absolutely last dance!

Joshua I better get back.

Judas See you.

JOSHUA *moves away and begins to dance with* PATRICIA. *The last dance is a very romantic arrangement.* JUDAS *disappears in the shadows.*

Bert Moody As we bid a fond farewell to our four years at Pontius Pilate High, let us remember to drive safely home, foresaking all opportunities to imbibe the grape and respecting the virtue of the virgins we walked in here with. The Roman Prefect has asked me to remind you that the city gates will be locked at one A.M. and not reopened until five A.M. You are warned. *Quo vadis, amigo?*

Music swells as ACTORS *disperse.* JOSHUA *and* PATRICIA *are making out in a parked car. The music coming from the radio is a quiet version of "Amazing Grace." We are aware of the glow of* JUDAS's *cigarette in the shadows.*

35

Joshua I love you, Patricia.

Patricia Those aren't my tits, Josh. These are my tits. Are You sure you've done this before?

Joshua Lots of times.

Patricia Ouch!

Joshua Sorry.

Patricia We don't have to do this.

Joshua But I want to.

Patricia I don't think Your heart is really in it. I saw what You were doing with that guy, Josh. It's okay. I understand. I mean, I'm not going to throw up or anything.

Joshua Would you like Me to take you home?

Patricia The one night of your life you're supposed to stay out all night and come home at dawn with sand in your hair and try to convince your parents "Of course I didn't go all the way" when of course that's exactly what you *did* do! Mine will never believe I'm still a virgin and it'll be true. This is what Mrs. McElroy means by dramatic irony.

Joshua I'm sorry.

Patricia You gotta stop saying that, Josh. It's getting to be a habit of Yours. I'm not going to let You humiliate me by taking me home now. We'll watch the sunrise. If You tell me Your biggest, deepest secret—the one You'd die if anyone else knew—maybe I'll tell You mine.

They get out of the car. In the starry night we can see other COUPLES *lying on blankets on the beach. It is as if the whole world is making love.*

Patricia So? I'm listening.

Joshua I hear hammering.

Patricia When? Right now? That's the surf.

Joshua All My life I've heard hammering. Like someone is building something and they never stop. Something for Me. And they're waiting for Me to what? I don't know.

Patricia If that's Your biggest secret, no wonder You're weird. Mine is I'm in love with Spider Sloan even though I also hate him. It's called ambivalence.

Joshua And sometimes I hear this voice. I never know when. It always says the same thing:

Judas (*from the shadows*) This is My son in whom I take much delight.

Patricia Who said that?

Judas Hello, Patricia. Spider's right over there, he's nailing Laurie Paulson.

Patricia I hate you. I hate you both.

PATRICIA *runs back to the bench.*

Judas (*after her*) It's not my fault he thinks you're the ugliest girl in town.

Joshua That was cruel.

Judas She'll get over it. Besides, maybe it's my nature.

Joshua I don't believe that. That's no one's nature.

Judas What's Your nature, Joshua?

Joshua I don't know. Kindness, I hope. Love. Respect for others.

Judas I believe You.

JUDAS *pulls* JOSHUA *toward him.*

Joshua You can come no closer to Me than My body. Everything else you will never touch. Everything important is hidden from you.

Josh Lucas as Judas and Anson Mount as Joshua

Judas Whatever.

JUDAS kisses JOSHUA. This time JOSHUA responds.

Patricia All my life I will remember that night and every time I do, I will be so sad and angry it turned out the way it did. I know that's selfish. I mean, He was Joshua, after all, but we didn't know that then and I was just Patricia Rudd at the time but I wanted someone to love me so badly that night. Put that down, Tiffany! How many times do I have to tell you, young lady! When your father gets home! Excuse me. Goddamnit, Tiffany!

Spider Sloan About five and a half years after that night (and yes, I plowed Laurie Paulson, who later married my best friend, Billy Brown—I'm godfather to their three kids) I was in the service, really drunk one night, and I let this queer blow me. He was down there doing it and I said, "Do you know

Joshua?" and he shook his head no. I thought they all knew one another. I said, "From up here you look like Joshua." I don't know what that makes me—it was one blow job for Christ's sake—but it doesn't make me one of them. Not a cocksucker but a cocksuckee, I guess. Nancy, where'd you hide my blue socks?

Peggy Powell What can I tell you? I certainly didn't know He was the son of God, if that's what you're asking. You don't decorate your high school gym for your senior prom or edit the yearbook with someone you think is the Messiah. He wasn't boyfriend material, that's for certain.

Mrs. McElroy I loved all my students. I can't pretend I had a favorite. I just wanted each of them to be true to himself (or herself) and reach his (or her) potential as a creative human being.

Dub He was. . . . What? I can't put it in words. I would come to weep many tears for how we treated Him.

Mrs. McElroy I was a high school English teacher. He was my student. One of many, many hundreds. I know how you would have liked me to say something else. I'm sorry.

All the ACTORS *save* JOSHUA *and* JUDAS *have returned to their places on the benches.* JOSHUA *and* JUDAS *are now young men.*

Judas Had Judas lived a long life, he would have forgotten that night—and the many other nights.

Joshua Liquid Gulf Coast nights . . .

Judas He and Joshua shared. Nights he wished—

Joshua We both wished—

Judas Would never end.

Joshua Maybe he would have forgotten the night we painted "J & J 4VR" on the water tower and the next day nobody knew who J and J were but us.

39

Judas But because he did not grow old, all he remembered was what he could not have, he longed for what he could not have, and he grew twisted and envious and afraid.

Judas But not yet. That is later in our story.

John Now began Joshua's many years of wandering. Years lost to us. He left no note. One morning, just like that, He was gone. Some say He went to China; others, India. I don't have to tell you where the Irish think he went. I personally don't think He ever left the state of Texas.

> JOSHUA *picks up his things and begins to hitchhike. The roar of big trucks passing Him by at high speeds is deafening.*

Truck Driver (*whizzing by*) Get a haircut!

Joshua (*after him*) Screw you!

Truck Driver #2 Hot enough for You, shithead?

Joshua I love you, too!

God Joshua, the time has come to leave Corpus Christi and begin Your life as the son of man.

Joshua What does it look like I'm doing? I'm way ahead of You.

God I'm sending You a messenger.

Truck Driver #3 Hello, sonny, going my way?

Joshua I am now.

Truck Driver #3 Hop in.

Joshua Thanks. What's that smell?

Truck Driver #3 Just a little patch of leprosy on my right arm here. Guess it's time to change the ol' air freshener. Tell me something: Am I on the right side of the road?

Joshua What's the matter? You blind?

Truck Driver #3 Not to worry, son. Blind since birth and behind the wheel since twelve. All's I need's my bearing and away we go. Hang on!

TRUCK DRIVER #3 puts the truck in gear and it roars off.

So where You headed?

Joshua Anywhere you take Me.

Truck Driver #3 Running away or running to?

Joshua Just running.

It quickly becomes night. The stars are blinding, the sky is midnight blue.

It got so cold all of a sudden!

JOSHUA shivers.

Truck Driver #3 That's the desert for you. This is the scary part of the trip. Miles and miles of desert up ahead. Nothing but sand and heat. Not a place you want to break down. I did once. Left me a changed man. I had to hug myself at night to stay warm and make my own shade at high noon. You ever been alone like that? It can drive a person crazy. I thought I saw Anita Ekberg offering me a glass of ice cold milk. She was a Swedish actress before Your time. Famous for her tits. I told her I loved her and she just laughed, the way all mirages mock and deceive us, and let the cold milk run down her creamy breasts and vanished, only to appear again on the next horizon. We all have mirages we chase after. Mine was flesh. Wonder what Yours'll be?

Joshua Why are you telling Me all this?

Truck Driver #3 Turn on the radio if You don't want me talking Your ear off. 'Course all You're gonna get this time of night is religious fanatics.

JOSHUA turns on the radio.

God's Voice This is My son in Whom I am well pleased.

Truck Driver #3 What did I tell You? Sounds like He's trying to tell You something.

JOSHUA turns off the radio.

That ain't gonna make His voice go away.

Joshua All my life I've heard it. I don't know what it means.

Truck Driver #3 He's saying He's well pleased with You.

Joshua How can He be pleased with Me when I am so displeased with Myself?

Truck Driver #3 He has given You the gift of healing. Touch me.

Joshua I don't want to touch you.

Truck Driver #3 Touch me!

TRUCK DRIVER #3 takes JOSHUA's hands and puts them on his eyes.

Thank You, Lord! I can see. My skin is smooth. The air is sweet. I am healed of all affliction. He has given You the greatest gift of all, son of God.

Joshua Don't call Me that! I'm not worthy.

Truck Driver #3 Then become worthy. Now get out. The world is waiting for You. Get out, I said!

JOSHUA gets out.

Joshua Who are you? Tell me.

Truck Driver #3 Ask a *hard* question next time. *Hasta luego, amigo!*

TRUCK DRIVER #3 is gone.

Joshua Wait! Don't leave Me here! I'll die out here. Is that what You want?

All the ACTORS *start to leave the stage.*

Where are you going? Wait. Come back! Don't leave me.

All the other ACTORS *have gone.* JOSHUA *is utterly alone in a pool of light that becomes the terrible burning desert.*

I'll wait. Someone else will come.

Pause. In the distance, we hear what sounds like a truck approaching.

Here comes someone. Stop! Slow down!

The sounds of a large truck barreling by JOSHUA *on the highway. The force of it sends* JOSHUA *flying.*

A mirage. The old man was right.

JAMES DEAN *appears. He wears a red windbreaker.*

James Dean You okay?

JAMES DEAN *helps* JOSHUA *up.*

Joshua Jimmy?

Jimmy Dean Where You headed?

Joshua I don't know.

Jimmy Anyplace is better than here. Somebody told me You saw *East of Eden* twelve times?

Joshua And *Rebel Without a Cause* ten.

Jimmy What about *Giant*?

Joshua Just once.

Jimmy What's wrong with *Giant*?

Joshua Nothing. It wasn't about Me.

Jimmy That's selfish.

Joshua I know.

Jimmy Not everything can be about You, Joshua.

Joshua Well, also you got old in it and died at the end.

Jimmy I didn't die. I was just dead drunk. (*He points.*) That's how I died. That Porsche with the buzzards sitting on it. You know how you're going to die?

Joshua No.

Jimmy You want to know?

Joshua No.

Jimmy What's wrong?

Joshua And God so loved the world He gave His only son to it.

Jimmy And He chose You?

Joshua I don't want to be different, Jimmy. I want to be like everyone else. I want to be happy.

Jimmy Sure You do.

Joshua I want to love someone.

Jimmy I know, I know.

Joshua I want someone to love Me. I want My life to matter.

Jimmy Come here.

> JUDAS *appears from upstage and joins* JOSHUA, *who teters at the edge of the void.*

Judas Don't worry. I've got You. It's a long way down.

Jimmy Now what do You see down there, shimmering in the sun?

Joshua A great city.

Anson Mount as Joshua and Josh Lucas as Judas

Jimmy Welcome to Your new kingdom, Your Majesty. How do You like it?

Joshua It's amazing.

Jimmy Just say the word and it's Yours.

Joshua What do I have to do?

Jimmy Almost nothing.

Joshua Tell me. What?

Jimmy It's so little it's hardly worth mentioning.

Joshua What?

Jimmy A moment later and You won't even remember You've done it.

Joshua What?

45

Jimmy Deny You're the son of God.

Joshua But I am the son of God.

Jimmy Deny it anyway. I did and look at me, King of the World! You will feel nothing but Yourself. Your needs, Your pleasures. It's a small price for all that. Are You ready?

Joshua It would be a lie.

Jimmy Think long and hard, Joshua. I offer You all the pleasures of His earthly kingdom. He offers You a wooden cross.

A CRUCIFIED MAN *appears in* JOSHUA's *delirium.*

See Yourself, Joshua. That is His promise. Down there is mine. Choose.

Joshua I have chosen. I want to see God. I want to know Him. You are no friend of Mine. Get thee behind Me.

JUDAS *flings* JOSHUA *off the precipice.*

Judas Satan cursed Him and was gone. He would seek Judas to do his work.

Peter Joshua had endured His time in the desert. He had embraced His destiny. His time had come. He would live as the son of God in peace and love with all men. He had found His way to the city and—I'm happy to say:

All Us!

All the ACTORS *become this great city. Lots of noise and activity.*

Peter Fish! Get your fresh fish here. I have eels. I have snapper! I have lung! I've got perch. I've got scrod. I've got rhythm.

JOSHUA *approaches, weak from hunger.*

I've got a customer. Hi.

Joshua They look good.

Peter They are good. I caught them myself. What can I get You?

Joshua I don't have any money.

Peter You and everybody else. How do You expect to live?

Joshua I don't know. The kindness of strangers.

Peter I wouldn't count on it.

Joshua The Bible says the Lord will provide.

Peter I'm not the Lord. Nothing's for free.

PETER *resumes hawking.*

I have squid! I have sole!

PETER *stops.*

Are You just going to stand there like that?

Joshua It's a free country.

Peter Until some Roman centurion cracks Your skull open because he doesn't like the way You looked at him. When was the last time you ate?

Joshua I don't remember.

Peter All right, I'll give You one. They're just going to spoil anyway.

Joshua Are you always this generous?

Peter Almost never. Don't tell anyone. I don't want to get a reputation.

PETER *puts one fresh fish in a basket and hands it to* JOSHUA.

Joshua Thank you. What's your name?

Peter Peter. Simon Peter.

A POOR WOMAN *approaches.*

Poor Woman/ James the Less Please, sir? It's not for me. My children are starving.

Peter See what You started?

Poor Woman We'll take anything.

Peter What do you think I'm running? I'm a fishmonger, not a charity. Go to the poorhouse. They'll feed you.

Joshua Here, take mine.

JOSHUA *gives her His fish.*

Poor Woman Thank You, young man.

Peter What are you doing? She's a beggar.

Joshua So am I.

Peter She's not one of us.

Joshua She is all of us. You say you have children?

Poor Woman Five.

Joshua What are their names?

Poor Woman Antony, Julia, Mark, Flor, and Joseph, he's the littlest.

JOSHUA *takes five fish from the basket* PETER *gave him.*

Joshua This is for Antony, this is for Julia, one for Mark, here's Flor's, and this one is for little Joseph. My father is called Joseph.

Poor Woman God bless You!

The POOR WOMAN *spontaneously throws her arms around Him. She exits.*

Peter I gave You one fish. You gave her five.

Joshua You would have given her none.

Peter It was a miracle.

Joshua I asked and they were given. You could have given her five hundred fish. You said so yourself: they'll only spoil. Who were you saving them for? You have a big heart, Simon Peter. You opened it to Me. Open it to everyone. There's room in there for all of us. Listen with this . . .

JOSHUA *puts His hand on* PETER's *heart.*

—not with what others have told you you must do. When we don't love one another, we don't love God.

PETER *puts his hand on* JOSHUA's *heart.*

Do you hear Him?

Peter I hear Your heart beating.

Joshua Then you hear God.

Peter I'm trembling.

Joshua Me, too. You are My brother. If you are wretched, I am wretched, too.

They embrace.

Peter (*to us*) Was it really like this, are you wondering? Yes, it was. I think it always is when Joshua or Jesus or whatever you want to call Him is revealed to you. The false images fall away. In your heart there is a sudden burning sensation, a fire.

Joshua We will go where God the father takes us. We will teach His word. Make it new again. Will you come with Me?

John And Peter put down his nets and went with Him. There were a lot of free fish that day! Soon, very soon, in fact, there were five of us. I remember I was in a park. This young guy was speaking. He had a nice little crowd. I started writing down what He said.

Joshua Love the Lord God your father by loving one another. That is where He is, in each of us, not in temples or false idols. (*To* JOHN) You don't have to write down what I say. You're not in school. Do it! Open your hearts to each other. I was alone for so long. Now I have a brother in this man.

JOSHUA *puts his arm around* PETER.

But I'm greedy. I want more.

Peter We adored Him. We would have followed Him to the ends of the earth. He was our leader.

Joshua (*protesting*) God is our leader. I'm just this guy like you. No better, no worse. I can't gut a fish, Peter, and I don't think I ever want to. I couldn't begin to cut someone's hair, Thaddeus. God knows, I can't sing. You've all heard Me. But when you do, Simon, you're singing for Me, saying things I can't. John writes down everything I say, which is good, because I don't remember half the time. We're each special. We're each ordinary. We're each divine.

Thomas What about me? You left me out.

Joshua I'm sorry. You're very special, Thomas.

Thomas Thank you.

Joshua You're very ordinary.

Thomas Thank you.

Joshua And you're very divine.

ANDREW *erupts from his place on the bench.*

Andrew Fuck you, fuck you. Help me. Eat shit. Die. Help me. Fuck you, fuck you. Help me!

Peter Be careful! He's possessed by a demon. Get away from us!

Andrew Help me, please. Heal me.

Joshua Let Me hold you, brother.

Andrew Sir, if only (fuck you, fuck you) You will (fuc[...] mother, fuck your father), You can drive the evil spirit [...] (fuck God!) and make me clean again.

Joshua I will try.

JOSHUA *holds* ANDREW *fiercely to Him.*

Father, if it is Thy will, let Me drive the demon from this man. Satan, be gone.

Judas And he was.

Peter Look, there he goes!

Joshua Be clean again, as you were as a child.

Andrew It's stopped. It's a miracle.

BARTHOLOMEW *and* JAMES *come from their place on the bench.*

Bartholomew That wasn't medicine. That was witchcraft.

Joshua Why are you so angry, brother?

Bartholomew I'm not Your brother. I'm a doctor. Two hours ago, a young man died in my arms at the hospital. His skin was yellow. He weighed ninety-three pounds. He was going to be a doctor. "Help me," he said. His eyes were still bright. They looked right at me. "Help me." I couldn't save him with all my skills and medicines and love and neither could You. We don't need Messiahs. We need cures.

Joshua I have no answer for you.

Bartholomew Then why should I follow You?

Joshua You are a man who has lost faith.

Bartholomew What planet have you been living on? We've all lost faith.

James He didn't mean that.

Bartholomew Don't tell me what I mean, James. I'm not one of your students.

BARTHOLOMEW goes back to the bench and sits.

James I'm sorry. He hasn't slept in three days. He's a good man.

Joshua I believe that, James.

JAMES joins BARTHOLOMEW.

Well, so be it. We've got a lot of work to do.

Simon But it never felt like work.

Thomas We did what are called good deeds. With Joshua it seemed impossible there could be any other kind.

John Of course we got into trouble, too. People were listening to Him and there were more and more of us. The authorities didn't like that.

James the Less Finally someone was telling the truth. We weren't free. We were slaves of Rome. My first night with Him and we all ended up in jail.

Matthew That's when you all decided you needed a good lawyer.

Joshua No, that's when you decided we needed a good lawyer, Matthew.

Thaddeus And then there were the Saturday nights. We had some pretty wonderful Saturday nights.

The other DISCIPLES have brought forward a bright and gaudy Wurlitzer juke box. EVERYONE starts dancing. All the DISCIPLES are present—even the ones who haven't "met" JOSHUA yet. They dance alone and/or in appropriate combinations: JAMES THE LESS and MATTHEW, BARTHOLOMEW and

JAMES. *High above them all is a go-go boy. It is* PHILIP. *He has bells on his feet.*

Judas Want to dance?

Joshua Judas!

Judas I thought it was You. How long has it been? Let me get a look at You. You're a man now.

Joshua We both are.

Judas The boy has become a master.

Joshua Are you rich?

Judas Can't You tell?

Joshua Are you powerful?

Judas Beyond my wildest dreams. I own three restaurants. Just try to get a reservation. What about You?

Joshua I'm happy.

Judas I believe You. Your eyes are shining.

Joshua So are Yours.

Judas I'm happy to see You.

    JUDAS takes a hit on a popper.

I'm on my way to oblivion. Care to join me?

Joshua You don't need that.

Judas You're right; I don't.

    JUDAS takes another hit. PHILIP *approaches.*

Joshua Who's that?

Thomas Ignore him, Josh. He's bad news.

James He's not interested, Philip.

Philip You're all interested. I have bells on my ankles. Hear them? Tinkle, tinkle, tinkle. I'm ringing them just for You, Joshua. Tinkle, tinkle, tinkle.

Peter Ignore him, Josh.

Philip Can't You speak for Yourself, master? Don't You want a little slave boy tonight?

Joshua They told Me you were a hustler.

Philip I am. They all want me, that's why they hate me. I know who likes it rough, who likes it sweet, who likes it fast, who likes it slow. I bet You I know how You like it, Joshua.

Peter Get away from us, you little disease-ridden, filthy whore! You're talking to the son of God.

Joshua And He is listening. Why are you so quick to judge others? All of you.

Philip It's all right. I don't hear them anymore. You want me, don't you, Joshua?

Joshua I don't have any money.

Philip What can You pay me with?

Joshua My life. I have nothing else to give you.

Philip I could take that from You. It wouldn't be the first time.

Others Don't go with him! He's dangerous! He's sick!

JOSHUA *and* PHILIP *disappear through the* OTHERS. *The disco music stops.*

Philip Get undressed. You got five minutes. Did You hear what I said?

Joshua I love you.

Philip Say what?

Joshua I love you, Philip.

Philip I love You, too, Charlie. I hope You have rubbers. I'm positive.

Joshua I said I love you.

Philip Hey! Don't fuck with me. You love the idea of telling someone like me You love them. It makes You feel good. Love this.

Joshua I think I can heal you. I think I can make you well.

Philip I think You can suck my dick now, faggot.

JOSHUA *goes to* PHILIP *and takes him by both arms and looks directly into his eyes.*

Joshua Father, heal this man.

Philip Fuck You.

Joshua Let these hands make him well. Give him back his life.

Philip Fuck You, I said.

Joshua You are healed, Philip.

Philip I wish I could believe that.

Joshua Then do. As you believe, so shall you be. You are healed, I say.

PHILIP *kneels before* JOSHUA. *His head is bowed.*

Philip I was going to beat the shit out of You and take Your wallet.

Joshua There wasn't anything in it.

Philip I am not worthy to kiss your feet.

Peter None of us are.

Philip And from the moment these lips kissed His feet, Philip was happy. It didn't matter who he'd been. He was well again, body and soul.

Peter I'm sorry, Philip, I wronged you. We all did.

One by one all the ACTORS *cross to* JOSHUA *and kiss His feet.*

SIMON *sings a hymn in his beautiful, clear, light tenor until it is his turn.*

BARTHOLOMEW *and* MATTHEW *stand apart from the others now.*

Joshua Do you believe, Bartholomew, I have the power to do what you want but cannot? As you believe, let it be.

Bartholomew Is it possible?

Joshua You saw with your own eyes.

James We did, Bart, we saw.

Bartholomew Let me heal my brothers. That is all I ask.

BARTHOLOMEW *prostrates himself before* JOSHUA *and kisses His feet.*

Peter Are you with us?

Judas Sure, why not?

He kisses JOSHUA's *feet. Now only* MATTHEW *stands apart.*

Matthew I'm sorry, gentlemen, but I have a lot of trouble kissing someone's feet.

James the Less Joshua isn't someone.

Matthew I think it's degrading. It reeks of servitude. It's the language of slaves.

James the Less That's not what it's saying.

JOSHUA *has come to where* MATTHEW *is standing.*

Joshua I love you, Matthew.

Matthew You're not better than me, Joshua. I can't accept that.

Joshua I am less than you.

Anson Mount as Joshua and Matthew Mabe as Philip

JOSHUA prostrates Himself and kisses MATTHEW's feet.
MATTHEW puts his face in his hands and weeps.

John Matthew never went back to his office at the law firm. Instead, he gave away everything he owned. His home. His car. His father's ring. Everything.

Peter We were twelve.

The DISCIPLES come together, happily embracing each other. Music. Laughter.

John The days that followed were glorious. We lived hand to mouth but we didn't care. We never went hungry. Someone always fed us.

Thomas I loved the miracles, even if I didn't get one of my own. Walk! See! Hear! I couldn't do them, of course, none of us could, but I loved watching Joshua.

Bartholomew We slept in fields. I saw my first eclipse. I helped a woman give birth: amazing.

Peter All thirteen of us, arm in arm, we were quite a sight. We were so fucking cool it hurt.

Joshua (*an admonishment*) Peter.

Peter Right. (But we were!)

Simon There was an old man named Lazarus. He'd been dead for six days and was starting to smell to high Heaven. He had a wife and six daughters. I wish you could have heard the racket they were making.

And we do as the DISCIPLES *become the* WAILING WOMEN. *They are* loud. THOMAS *is* LAZARUS.

Joshua Arise, Lazarus.

Simon I think this was one of the practical miracles. I mean, there was no big reason for it. Lazarus wasn't a big cheese or even an especially nice guy. Joshua just couldn't stand the noise.

Increased wailing from the women.

Joshua Shut up, women. Thank you. I say Lazarus, arise.

LAZARUS *suddenly sits up.*

Lazarus What is the matter with you? You'd think you'd seen a ghost!

Joshua You have been asleep, Lazarus—not for six days but for all the years of your life. Now live as if your very life depended on it.

Lazarus How do I live? Teach me.

Joshua Be awake every moment and give thanks to God the Father for it. Give back as much—no, more!—than you have been given. Laugh. Fill your lungs with His good air and pray. You have all forgotten to pray.

Lazarus (*kneeling, head lowered*) God, forgive this wretched sinner.

Joshua Not like that: on your knees, head bowed, your eyes closed! You're not afraid of Him. Like this: standing tall, eyes open, smiling even, your arms open to His love. This is how we talk to God. Our Father which art in heaven, hallowed be Thy name. Thy kingdom come. Thy will be done on earth, as it is in Heaven. Give us this day our daily bread. And forgive us our debts as we forgive our debtors. And lead us not into temptation, but deliver us from evil: For Thine is the kingdom and the power and the glory, for ever. Alleluia!

All Alleluia!

James the Less Everywhere we went we found great crowds awaiting us at every bend in the road.

Simon People were desperate for some message. They had lost their way.

Philip Young people flocked to Him. He understood them. They hung on His every word.

Joshua Love thy neighbor as thyself.

Thaddeus/Centurion Sir, if I may.

Bartholomew (*sarcastically*) A Roman centurion! Have you come to arrest us? Or just beat us up this time? Be careful, we have a very good lawyer now.

Joshua Why are you such bastards? What little love you have. This man's eyes are red from weeping. Forgive My friends. Speak. You are welcome.

Centurion My wife is dying. You're our only hope.

Joshua I will come.

Philip Don't go. It's a trap.

James the Less He's one of the enemy.

Joshua Such words make you Mine. James the Less was for your stature but it is also for your heart. Lead the way.

Centurion Sir, we are not worthy to have You in our home. You have only to say the word and she will be cured.

Joshua Go home. Your wife is waiting for you. As you believe, so let it be.

CENTURION *goes.*

Truly, I tell you, nowhere in Israel have I found such faith, not even among My own disciples.

James the Less What You teach comes easily from the lips, but so much harder from the heart. Help me.

Joshua Love the Lord thy God with your heart and soul. Forgive your greatest enemy.

James the Less I can't.

Joshua You must. I require mercy, not sacrifice. I do not say seventy times but seven times seventy. Nothing more, nothing less.

James the Less I'm not ready.

Joshua Would that we were all as honest as this man.

Bartholomew It was the same afternoon He preached the Sermon on the Mount. It seemed there was nothing He couldn't do. We were coming home from it, home that week being under an oak tree by a creek, when we encountered the same centurion.

The CENTURION *returns.*

Joshua There's our friend. How is she?

Centurion I was too late. She was dead.

Joshua I'm sorry.

Peter It was God's will, Josh. You said so Yourself.

Joshua Well, it wasn't mine! (*Then*) I'm so ashamed. Forgive Me, all of you.

Peter And from that time there were fewer miracles of the flesh, but more and more miracles of the heart, simple acts that were worth three dozen exorcisms.

James Bartholomew and I had wanted our union blessed for a long time—some acknowledgment of what we were to each other.

Bartholomew We asked, Josh. They said it was against the law and the priests said it was forbidden by Scripture.

James "If a man lies with a man as with a woman, both of them have committed an abomination; they shall be put to death, their blood is upon them."

Joshua Why would you memorize such a terrible passage? "And God saw everything that He had made, and behold it was very good." I can quote Scripture as well as the next man. God loves us most when we love each other. We accept you and bless you. Who's got a ring?

James Will You do it?

Joshua If you say nobody else will!

Bartholomew Out here? Someone might see.

Joshua Where would you be married, Bartholomew? Down a dark hole? We will marry you in broad daylight under the canopy of Heaven in the eyes of God and for all men to see. I said, who's got a ring?

Philip You can borrow mine. Okay, okay, *have!*

Joshua Who's got another one? Judas?

Judas Sorry, I can't.

Thomas Take mine.

Peter The priests will have something to say about this, Joshua.

Joshua The priests have something to say about everything. Let's have some music. Who wants to give the groom away?

John I will!

James I'm the groom!

Joshua Who wants to give the other groom away?

James the Less I'll do it.

JAMES *and* BARTHOLOMEW *stand in front of* JOSHUA.

Joshua It is good when two men love as James and Bartholomew do and we recognize their union. No giggling back there! Now, take each other's hand. Love each other in sickness and health. Respect the divinity in your partner, Bartholomew. Cherish the little things in him, James, exalt in the great. May the first face you see each morning and the last at night always be his. I bless this marriage in Your name, Father. Amen. Now let's all get very, very drunk.

Bartholomew You are truly the Messiah, son of the living God.

MATTHEW *enters as the* HIGH PRIEST.

Joshua Have you come to bless this marriage, too, father?

High Priest It is one thing to preach your perversions to ignorant and sentimental men and women such as yourselves, but such travesties of God's natural order will never be blessed in the House of the Lord by one of His ordained priests.

Joshua This is the House of the Lord. I ordain Myself.

High Priest You have broken every commandment.

Joshua You are hypocrites. You are liars. You have perverted My father's words to make them serve your ends. I despise you.

JOSHUA sends the HIGH PRIEST flying with a single blow.

Thomas Joshua, You struck a priest.

Joshua And I'll do it again. All who do not love all men are against Me!

Thomas But You said we must always turn the other cheek.

Joshua I must have been in a very good mood. Do not take everything I say so seriously.

The high spirits of the wedding celebration have been quickly deflated.

Peter Joshua.

Joshua Not now, Peter.

Peter Let me.

Joshua I said not now. Go out and preach the Gospel. That is what disciples do.

John We don't know how.

Joshua You don't know how to speak the truth?

Thomas They want to hear You.

Joshua The Word is the Word, not the man who speaks it. What an unbelieving and perverse generation. What will you do when I am no longer with you?

Judas I'll stay with Him.

The other DISCIPLES disperse. JOSHUA puts his head in JUDAS's lap.

That's better.

JUDAS strokes JOSHUA's head.

Joshua I get so angry.

Judas I know. Ssshh. Sleep now.

From the left: Josh Lucas, Troy Sostillio, Sean Dugan, Michael Irby, Anson Mount, Michael Hall, Jeremy Shamos, Christopher Fitzgerald, and Ken Leung

Sounds of crickets. Night. The campfire is very low. SIMON *stands looking down at* JOSHUA *sleeping in* JUDAS's *lap.*

Simon One night we were around the fire. Just the two of us. He'd just performed the miracle of the loaves and fishes. Five loaves and two fish fed five thousand men, not counting the women and children. Amazing! And twelve baskets were left over. I remember an owl hooting and thinking I'd never seen so many stars, so much stuff up there to wonder about. And for what seemed like an eternity, the two of us were one. Afterward, He said the strangest thing.

Joshua (*murmuring in His sleep*) You can come no closer to Me than your body, Simon. Everything else you will never touch. Everything important is hidden from you.

Judas He said the same thing to me when we were boys together on a beach in Corpus Christi.

Simon What did He mean?

Judas I don't know.

Simon Good night, Judas.

Judas Good night, Simon. (*To us*) What will you give me to betray Him to you? You know my price. Thirty pieces of silver. Not much for a place in history. Most of you will pass away quietly in your beds, or gasping for air in some miserable hospital, and your goings will be as unremarkable as your lives. Think about it.

> MATTHEW/HIGH PRIEST *tosses a bag of coins that lands in front of* JUDAS.

High Priest Thirty pieces of silver. You boys make it very easy for us.

Judas Thank you, father, we try.

High Priest But this one, He's a dangerous man.

Judas What is His crime?

High Priest Blasphemy.

Judas Because He says He's the son of God?

High Priest No, because He says you're the son of God as well.

Judas We're all the son of God.

High Priest Unless you're looking for trouble, I would keep that to myself. The son of God is a cocksucker? I don't think so. We need sinners.

Judas Last chance for immortality; going, going, gone. Sold to the fag haters in priest's robes.

High Priest Good Passover, Judas Iscariot.

Judas Happy Easter to you, rabbi.

HIGH PRIEST goes. JOSHUA wakes up in JUDAS's lap.

Judas Hello, sleepyhead.

Joshua Where is everybody?

Judas They're all sleeping. No one here but us chickens. You fell asleep in my lap, just like old times.

Joshua I couldn't dance. Didn't know how to dress. No car. What did you ever see in Me?

Judas Everything.

Joshua Are you crying?

Judas I never cry, You know that. When did You ever see me cry?

Joshua Will you cry when they kill Me?

Judas Nobody's going to kill You.

Joshua Do you love Me?

Judas Yes.

Joshua Promise Me you'll be there when they do.

Judas I promise.

Joshua Then let's go home and end this.

Judas Corpus Christi.

Joshua Corpus Christi.

A burst of joyful music. The other DISCIPLES get to their feet. They wave palms and sing. Some of them whirl like dervishes. JOSHUA rides on THADDEUS's back. A delirious pandemonium.

Disciples (*variously*) Hail, Joshua! Hail, the son of man! Hail, the new Messiah!

Simon How does it feel to be home? You left in shame, return in triumph.

Joshua Nothing's changed yet everything's different.

People Hail! Hail! Hail!

Joshua Listen!

Sudden, utter silence with the sweep of His hand.

The hammering. It's stopped. Their work is done. The trap is set.

Philip/Carpenter In Your honor, for Passover, I have fashioned a table for You and Your disciples. That is the hammering You heard.

Joshua My father was a carpenter. They tell Me he was a good one.

The DISCIPLES bring out a long table.

Carpenter A good carpenter is worth his weight in gold. A man who can do something with his hands. Anyone can preach about love. But it takes a man to build a good, solid table.

Joshua We need a room to celebrate Passover.

Philip It has been prepared for You, master. Everything is just as it should be.

John The supper. We did not know it was to be the last one.

The stage picture should look like Da Vinci's.

Thaddeus We were in that part of Corpus called Gethsemane. The meal that night was delicious. Peter and James outdid themselves on the lamb.

Anson Mount as Joshua and Josh Lucas as Judas

Peter The secret is all in the marinade.

James And slow roasting. Slow, slow, slow.

Thomas Josh, there's a woman outside who says she is Your mother.

Joshua Tell her I have no mother. You are My mother and father and brothers and sisters. You are My family now. We are all mother, father, brothers, and sisters, each to the other. Now do you understand?

Andrew We looked at each other and we did.

Philip It was breathtaking.

James the Less A perfect moment.

Bartholomew A defining one.

Thaddeus A moment later and He took away our breath again.

Joshua One of you will betray Me this very night.

Thomas You're joking. He's joking!

Philip He's not.

Matthew Surely You don't mean one of us, Josh?

Joshua One who has shared many meals with Me. One who has lain with Me. One who has said he loves Me and knows that I love him.

Thomas That could be any one of us. See? I told you He was joking.

Joshua Alas for that man. It would be better for that man if he had never been born.

Simon Is it I, Lord?

John Is it I?

Matthew Is it me, Josh?

Thomas Not I, Lord, surely?

James the Less It could never be me.

Peter Not I, Josh.

Joshua No, but before the cock crows you will betray Me three times this night, Peter.

Peter I will cut off both my hands first.

Bartholomew Is it one of us?

James You married us.

Philip Me, Joshua?

Thaddeus I know what you're all thinking—he's just a silly hairdresser—but it's not going to be me.

Andrew Is it I?

Judas Is it I, Lord?

Joshua Judas, you have said it. I have counted every hair on your head.

Judas You're drunk, Josh. Who would betray the son of God and be damned for all eternity? He's drunk, guys. It's the wine talking.

Joshua When I am gone.

Judas No one's going anywhere. Can we have some music, Simon? A little Bo Diddley.

> SIMON *obliges. A festive mood struggles to reestablish itself.* JOSHUA *speaks over it.*

Joshua I say when I am gone I will always be with you.

Thomas That doesn't even make sense, Josh. How can You be with us if You're gone?

Joshua Take this bread and eat it in remembrance of Me. This bread is My body. Take this wine and drink. It is My blood.

> *Hilarity from the* OTHERS. *Some of them start a bread fight. Others are gurgling wine.*

Thaddeus Yada-yada-yada!

Philip Take this saltshaker. It is my life.

Peter Eat this knife. It is my gallbladder.

Andrew I want to dance. Everybody dance.

> *Some of the* APOSTLES *already are.*

Simon I'm crocked to the gills!

James the Less We all are. Ain't it terrific?

Thaddeus Happy Chanukah everyone!

Thomas It's Passover, you ape.

Matthew Who's counting?

Thaddeus Who are you calling an ape?

All the APOSTLES are clowning around, dancing, standing on the table, having a terrific time. Only JOSHUA and JUDAS remain still at the table. JOSHUA stands up.

Joshua My appointed time is near. I am going out to the garden to pray. Will you wait up for Me?

Andrew If we don't run out of wine and music!

Philip Sure we will, Josh.

Judas I'll come with You.

The other APOSTLES recede upstage as JOSHUA and JUDAS cross down to the Garden of Gethsemane.

Judas I'll be right over here.

JUDAS sits apart from JOSHUA. JOSHUA prays.

Joshua Father, I'm frightened. My hands are shaking. My stomach is so tight I can hardly breathe. I wipe My brow of sweat and it's blood. I'm angry, too! I don't want to die. Let this cup pass from Me. Don't make Me drink from it. I chose to be Your son. I can *un*choose.

A burst of music and laughter comes from the APOSTLES within.

Why must I die for them? They don't deserve what You ask of Me. Will it hurt? I asked You a question: Will it hurt when the nails pierce the palms of My hands?

Silence.

71

Why don't You answer Me?

Silence.

Take Me to You soon.

JOSHUA goes to where JUDAS has been waiting for Him.

Judas Did He tell You He loved You?

Joshua No. He didn't say anything. I'm ready. Are you?

The other ACTORS are lying on the floor, as if passed out from too much food and wine.

Joshua Couldn't you even wait up with Me one night? This night of all the others?

Now there are three loud knocks on the door, as at the very beginning of the play. The DISCIPLES wake up in panic. They scatter and "hide," i.e., they turn away from the playing area and become other characters again. Only JOSHUA and JUDAS remain.

Judas You brought this on Yourself, son of man.

Joshua So did you, Judas.

James the Less Which one of you calls Himself the son of man and the Messiah?

Judas I recognize You as Jesus of Galilee, known as Joshua of Corpus Christi, the son of man and my true Redeemer.

JUDAS kisses JOSHUA. JOSHUA kisses him back, hard.

James the Less Take Him.

JOSHUA is seized and surrounded by the OTHERS. PETER is the only one of the APOSTLES to step forward to defend JOSHUA. His sword is drawn.

Peter Anyone who touches this man answers to Simon Peter.

Soldier I'm quaking in my boots!

Anson Mount as Joshua in the garden of Gesthemane

PETER strikes the SOLDIER with his sword.

Ow!

Peter Who's next?

Soldier You cut off my ear.

Peter (*ready for the next one*) Come on, come on!

Soldier You cut off my fucking ear.

Peter I'll cut off your fucking balls!

Joshua Put up your sword, Peter. All who live by the sword shall die by the sword. Don't you think I could call a hundred angels to defend Me if I wanted?

He goes to the wounded SOLDIER.

Here.

Soldier Get away from me!

JOSHUA puts His hand on the SOLDIER's head and restores his ear.

Joshua God be with you, brother. (*To SOLDIERS*) I'm ready.

John The man was much amazed.

Soldier Holy shit!

John As were we all. Before we knew it, they had taken Him. Except for Peter, we never saw Him again. We were cowards. We fled. How quickly it all ended.

Judas What happens next is awful and beggars all description. I think we should stop here, gentlemen.

Philip You began it, Judas. Now tell it to the end.

PHILIP thrusts a Bible at JUDAS, who reads from it with growing difficulty and anguish.

Judas "They bound Him and mocked Him. Then did they spit in His face and buffet Him. And others smote Him with the palms of their hands, saying:

Bartholomew Prophesy unto us, Thou Christ, who is he that smote Thee? Smack!

Thaddeus Was it me? Smack!

Simon Or was it me? Smack!

Thaddeus/ Bartholomew/Simon Or maybe it was all three of us? Smack, smack, smack!!!

Judas When the morning was come, all the chief priests took counsel against Him to put Him to death and they delivered Him to Pontius Pilate, the governor."

Philip/Pilate What are the charges against Him?

Andrew/Pilate's Wife Have nothing to do with this man, husband. I had a dream of Him last night. He is innocent.

Pilate Art thou a queer then?

Joshua Thou sayest I am.

Pilate What do You say?

Joshua To this end I was born and for this cause I came into the world, that I should bear witness unto the truth.

Pilate The truth! What is truth? I'll tell You: It's a word and nothing more. Poof! It's gone. If I were You, I'd save myself, fairy.

Joshua I am saved, friend. Are you?

Pilate You are arrogant.

Pilate's Wife Have nothing to do with Him!

Pilate (*to the crowd*) I find in Him no fault but His damnable pride. But you have a custom that I should release one prisoner to you at Passover. Will you therefore that I release to you the queer or the thief, Barabbas?

All Not the queer, the thief. Barabbas! Barabbas! Barabbas!

Judas "And Barabbas was released to them."

Thaddeus/Barrabas (*kneeling before* PILATE) God bless you, sir! I'll remember you for this.

> THADDEUS/BARRABAS *kisses the hem of* PILATE's *robe, then stands.*

Then he got very drunk and went to a neighborhood they called Boys' Town and fucked his brains out—what was left of them.

Judas "And the soldiers took Him to their company quarters and stripped Him and bound Him to a pillar and scourged Him while others knelt and adored Him as the King of the Queers."

> DUB, SPIDER, *and* BILLY *surround* JOSHUA.

Dub Hi, Joshua. Remember us? I'm Dub. He's Spider.

Billy And I'm Billy.

During the following, JOSHUA is stripped, bound, and scourged. It's theatricalized/stylized but it's never pretty. We should feel His passion.

Bartholomew/Nun Now some of you, when you're bad, have been spanked at home by your mothers and fathers. And from time to time, here, at Christ the King School, I, too, have had to reprimand you, though lovingly, always very lovingly. Penny Williams, did you chew gum during Mass?

Simon Yes, sister.

Bartholomew You know what to do. Put your hand out. No, knuckle side up this time. This hurts me more than it hurts you. The good Lord did not invent straight rulers for such a purpose. Stop whimpering, Penny Williams. Take it like a man. Swat! But you know who it hurts even more than you or I? Jesus Christ, your Savior. That's who. Swat! He cries to Himself up in Heaven when He sees bad little girls like you chewing gum during the Holy Sacraments of His most holy Mass. Swat! Swat! Swat! Now, open your catechisms. Why did God make you, Timothy Sheahan?

Judas "And the soldiers plaited a crown of thorns and put it on His head."

James/Little Boy Sister Mary Margaret told us one of the thorns was so long it went right through His skull and came out in the middle of His right eye!

Judas "They put Him in a purple robe and gave Him a stick as a scepter and mocked Him and smote Him with their hands again."

PETER has been watching JOSHUA's torment in an agony of his own.

Peter Don't hurt Him!

Pharisee/James the Less His name is Simon Peter. He's one of them, too!

Peter Don't be ridiculous.

Matthew/Philistine I saw them dancing together at a club!

Peter I don't know what you're talking about.

Hypocrite/John He corrupted my children.

Peter Do I look like one of them? I despise Him!

He spits in JOSHUA'*s face.*

James Cock-a-doodle-do!

JOSHUA *just looks at* PETER.

Peter I had no choice! They would have killed us all.

Simon Cock-a-doodle-do!

Peter I'm Your rock. You said so Yourself. Someone has to spread the Word after You're . . .

He catches himself.

Bartholomew Cock-a-doodle-do!

Peter What would You have done?

All Crucify Him! Crucify Him!

Judas "And they took Jesus, Joshua, and led Him away."

A cross is brought out from behind the stage. It is put on JOSHUA'*s shoulders. He falls under the weight of it.*

John/Simon of Cyrenae Let me help You, brother.

Joshua What is your name, brother?

John Simon. Simon of Cyrenae.

JOHN *carries the cross for* JOSHUA *through a jeering throng.*

John Try not to stop. They'll only beat You harder.

Joshua I thought I saw My mother. There, in the distance. I was wrong.

MARY waves to her son. He doesn't see her.

Mary That last night, when Mary was told her son would not receive her, she did not understand. Her life had not been an easy one. Who would take care of her in her old age? She was no longer beautiful. Now she looked away and lowered her head when his eyes sought hers.

Judas "And they came to the place called Golgotha. The place of skulls because so many criminals' bodies lay unburied there. The crowd grew silent. They stripped Him of His garment, which was of a color purple to mock His divinity."

Thaddeus I got dibs on the purple dress!

Judas "They lay Him roughly down on the cross."

Joshua Oh!

Judas "And then they nailed Him to it."

THADDEUS strikes the first nail. JOSHUA screams in agony. THADDEUS drops the hammer.

Matthew Idiot!

MATTHEW picks up the hammer and drives in the second nail.

John/James the Less (*drops to his knees*) Our Father who art in Heaven.

Matthew Shut them up! Will somebody shut them up!

Judas "A third nail was driven into his feet."

MATTHEW drives in the third nail. Someone in the crowd faints. Thunder and lightning. A wind begins to build.

Matthew (*the SOLDIERS make ready to raise the cross*) One, two, three, heave!!

The cross is raised. For the first time we see how horribly JOSHUA *has been battered. Blood runs down His face and body. His eyes are half-swollen shut. It should be hard to look at Him.*

Blessed are the meek, for they shall . . . what was that, cowboy?

James the Less Architect, what have you done?

Joshua Father, forgive them: they know not what they do.

Judas "In the distance, on the horizon, He could see some of the disciples who were too frightened to come closer and His mother and His aunt and the Mary called the Magdalene. It was some comfort."

John He looks thirsty. Give Him something to cool His parched mouth.

Bartholomew Here you go, cowboy! A sponge soaked in vinegar.

Thaddeus Suck on that!

Judas "Two other criminals were put to death with Him. Crucified, one to each side."

SIMON and ANDREW stand to each side of JOSHUA, *their arms extended, as if they, too, were crucified.*

Andrew Hey, faggot! If I was the son of God I wouldn't be hanging here with my dick between my legs. Save us all if you're really Him.

Simon Don't listen to him.

Andrew You can't do it 'cause You're not! Fuck.

ANDREW bows his head and dies.

Simon If You are the son of God, remember me when You get to Heaven.

Joshua Brother, you shall be with Me in Paradise today.

79

Simon I believe You, brother.

> SIMON *bows his head and dies. There is a crash of thunder and a flash of lightning. We hear the loud howling of the wind.*

Judas "A savage darkness fell over the place. The earth shook and graves opened. The people fled in terror. What had they done?"

> JUDAS *looks to* JOSHUA.

Are you suffering, Joshua?

Joshua Horribly, horribly.

> JOSHUA *lets out a cry of agony.*

Eloi, Eloi, lama sabbacthani!

Judas Which is Hebrew and which means, "My God, My God, why have You forsaken Me?"

God This is My son with Whom I am well pleased.

Joshua Father, into Thy hands I commend My spirit.

> JOSHUA *dies. We hear three loud knocks.* JUDAS *takes up a piece of rope and looks at it. Gradually, the other* ACTORS *return to center stage.*

The Actor Playing John Our play is over but the end is still to come. All these things you have seen and heard are the first birth pangs of the new age. Hold yourselves ready, therefore, because the son of man will come at the time when you least expect Him.

The Actor Playing James the Less Look what they did to Him. Look what they did to Him.

The Actor Playing Judas Sometimes I mourn for Judas, too. I believe Joshua would have.

The Actor Playing Thaddeus Maybe other people have told His story better. Other actors. This was our way.

The Actor Playing Simon If we have offended, so be it.

The Actor Playing Bartholomew He loved every one of us. That's all He was about.

The Actor Playing James the Less Look what they did to Him.

The Actor Playing Matthew (*to us*) Peace be with you.

The Actor Playing Philip (*to us*) Good-bye. Thank you.

> *The* ACTORS *exit, making conversation, or not, as they go. One* ACTOR *remains. He kneels at the side of the cross. The house lights are turned up. The play is over.*

THE END

About the Author

Corpus Christi was named one of the best plays of 1998 by *Time* magazine. Terrence McNally won Tony Awards for Best Play for *Love! Valour! Compassion!* and *Master Class,* as well as Tony Awards for Best Book of a Musical for *Ragtime* and *Kiss of the Spiderwoman.* In addition, *Love! Valour! Compassion!* won the Drama Desk, Outer Critics Circle, and the New York Drama Critics' Circle awards for Best Play. His other plays include *A Perfect Ganesh; Lips Together, Teeth Apart; The Lisbon Traviata; Frankie and Johnny in the Clair de Lune;* and *It's Only a Play.* Earlier stage works include *Bad Habits, The Ritz, Where Has Tommy Flowers Gone?, And Things That Go Bump in the Night,* and the book for the musical *The Rink.* He has written a number of television scripts, including *Andre's Mother,* for which he won an Emmy Award. Mr. McNally has received two Guggenheim fellowships, a Rockefeller grant, a Lucille Lortel Award, and a citation from the American Academy of Arts and Letters. A member of the Dramatists Guild since 1970, Mr. McNally has been vice president since 1981. Terrence McNally was raised in Corpus Christi, Texas, in the 1950s.